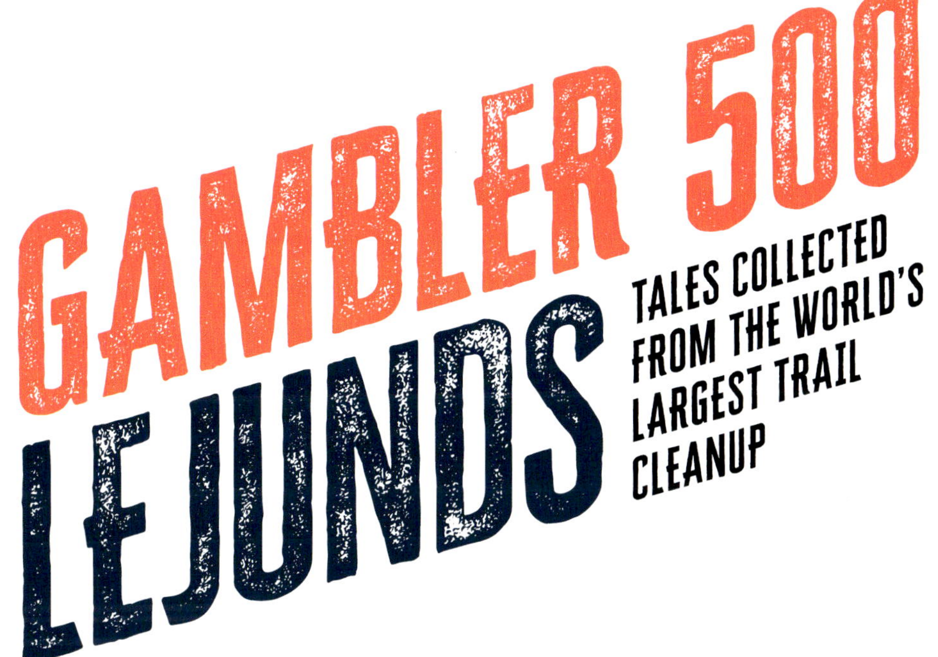

GAMBLER 500 LEJUNDS

TALES COLLECTED FROM THE WORLD'S LARGEST TRAIL CLEANUP

CLINT REQUA

Gibby with Nicole Poe. (*Nicole Poe*)

This book is dedicated to Jamie "Gibby" Gibson, as well as every other Gambler who reached the final waypoint at the end of life's long road and went on ahead. We'll see you in camp.

America Through Time is an imprint of Fonthill Media LLC
www.through-time.com
office@through-time.com

Published by Arcadia Publishing by arrangement with Fonthill Media LLC
For all general information, please contact Arcadia Publishing:
Telephone: 843-853-2070
Fax: 843-853-0044
E-mail: sales@arcadiapublishing.com
For customer service and orders:
Toll-Free 1-888-313-2665

www.arcadiapublishing.com

First published 2023

Copyright © Clint Requa 2023

ISBN 978-1-63499-481-1

Typeset in 10pt on13pt Sabon
Printed and bound in England

CONTENTS

ACKNOWLEDGMENTS

This collection of stories would not have been possible without the individual efforts of each person who took the time to type out their story, gather photographs, and send them to me. Words cannot adequately convey my gratitude. To the thousands of wonderful people who make up the Gambler community at large, thank you for being an overwhelmingly positive force in my life and the lives of countless others. In particular, I would like to single out Nicole Poe for taking to this project with unbelievable zeal, diligently working to see it completed despite my never having asked. I sincerely believe that this book would not have reached completion on time were it not for her invaluable assistance. Even among Gamblers, her star shines brightly.

My thanks as well to Tyler Herden and Pirate Johnny, who put this idea in my head in the first place. To Tanisha Mcintyre, Nate Fife, Bobby McAuslan, Indiana Allison, and Mercedes Streeter, who each provided their own compelling stories that ultimately could not be included in this volume. To Poncho Cole, Bj Snyder, and Stacy Dixon Kohon, who assisted with photos and detailed background information on their respective events. To Michael Orr, Ian Malone, Alex Janik, Todd Clark, Chris Ruiz, Dustin Leavitt and Tyler Buster—those Gamblers who have on multiple occasions helped me when I've been broken down or accepted my haphazard assistance when they did, and with whom I most regularly travel.

INTRODUCTION

My first foray into the world of "motorsports" was in 2016, when I managed to snag a seat with a team racing a worn-out BMW 3-Series in the 24 Hours of Lemons. For those not familiar with Lemons, the idea is to acquire a car for $500, cage it, and run it around a racetrack for a weekend in the (usually futile) hope that most of the important parts won't either fall off or catch fire. Being a naturally slow and cautious driver, I was poorly suited to conditions in which a lunatic in a Volkswagen Superbeetle named *Scrubby* might become one with my backside in the very likely event that I lifted off the throttle when I wasn't expected to.

In 2017, my focus shifted to Lemons Rally. Unlike the race series, there is no budget cap and far fewer rules. Participants are assigned points based on how objectively terrible their car is, given a list of checkpoints (which are both worth additional points and scattered across a large swath of the country), and left to their own devices for the next four to six days. The highest score wins the event. Being both the creative sort and curiously immune to becoming bored in a car, I excelled at this. Our first rally car was a Ford Aerostar minivan painted in spoof Martini Racing livery and christened the *Vancia S4 AeroStradale*.

In 2018, wanting to actually win something, I purchased a Mercedes SSK Gazelle kit car from a homeless man in Santa Cruz, California. The rickety fiberglass contraption was powered by an 80-hp Ford V6 and sat on a shortened Pinto chassis. We painted it to look like the *Thomas Flyer*, the car which won the infamous 1908 New York to Paris race. Described by 24 Hours of Lemons staffer and automotive journalist Eric Rood as sounding "like a herd of mountain goats smacking a canyon floor in a mass suicide; equal parts thump and bleat," the *Tortellini Flyer* nonetheless secured a first-place victory. Myself and two other grown men crammed ourselves, luggage, tools, spare parts, and a surprising amount of bread into a machine that could have fit all four wheels comfortably on a queen-sized mattress, then drove from California to Chicago and back along the famed Route 66.

The *Flyer* was miserable, but it was during the long process of preparing for the single worst thing that I would ever do to myself that I first heard about the Gambler 500. When a regional event passed too close to my house for me to ignore, I loaded up my

The second incarnation of Team Brawndo's E30, shown here at Buttonwillow Raceway in 2020. The original Brawndo E30 died a hideous death at this track in an accident which rendered the engine, gearbox, and body completely unsalvageable. Its replacement is powered by a Toyota 2JZ straight six, and was once described by professional driver Randy Pobst as "kinda scary, but fast!"

The Vancia S4 Aerostradale, loaded up for a surfing trip. Its ultimate fate remains a mystery.

The *Tortellini Flyer*, fully loaded. In terms of feats of equal parts ambition and stupidity, few can compare to enduring two weeks of interstate travel through torrential thunderstorms, freezing temperatures, and a complete lack of personal space, in this. Our backseat passenger, Ethan Manuputy, nearly succumbed to hypothermia in rural Iowa. We did win, though.

little fiberglass death trap and set off to find these mysterious Gamblers their overnight campsite. My immediate impression upon making contact with their ragtag convoy was that these people were unbelievably generous with their alcohol. I don't remember much else, except that my teetotaling teammate drove us home (I like to have fun, but I never condone drinking and driving). Apparently I made friends, though. I didn't know it at the time, but I had just met a group of people who would become, for all intents and purposes, a second family to me.

You don't need to be born with a wrench in your hand or a hole in your head to be a Gambler, but it does certainly help. The series was started in Oregon by all-around nice guy Tate Morgan and a few friends in 2014. Initially conceived as little more than a fun and creative way to kill a weekend, in the years since, the Gambler has grown exponentially. Regional groups have popped up everywhere from the series' home state to the rugged shores of Iceland. A whole menagerie of colorful characters, dubbed 'Lejunds' by those in the know, have carved out a niche for themselves as larger-than-life avatars of the Gambler spirit. Participants swap trading cards of noteworthy figures in the community while throwing back swigs of Gambler 500 whiskey around the campfire.

Trunk nachos at OG 2022. This Lancia Beta coupe was resurrected over the span of eight months in what can only be described as a feat of automotive necromancy. As of this publication, it remains the only Lancia to have ever made it to a Gambler event, most of which it spent acting as a dispenser of cheap wine and ferrying people between HooptieX camp and the main stage.

The original event—or "OG Gambler"—held every summer in central Oregon draws thousands of people from across North America. Collectively, the Gambler community has removed over 1 million pounds of trash from America's national forests. Along the way, they've partnered with companies such as O'Reilly Autoparts, Leatherman Tools, and Ford Motor Company to promote responsible land stewardship. They have also, bafflingly, earned a cease-and-desist notice from MeowMix cat food.

Putting into words the unique blend of comradery and chaos, unstoppable force of automotive destruction and borderline-militant reverence for public lands should by all rights be an impossible task. Gambler is big. Huge, in fact, and it's a million different things to thousands of different people. Perhaps that's part of why I spent eight months out of the year in which I was supposed to be compiling this book doing literally anything else. Perhaps that is also why I decided that this needed to be a group effort.

Within these pages, you will find stories, anecdotes, and photos, all submitted by Gamblers from around the United States. Each chapter puts the spotlight not only on an individual Gambler, but also the regional event from which their story is told. Friends, strangers, Stanley Gamblerton, every individual in the Gambler 500 community has a tale to tell. Listen, and let the words within this book become your own Bible of bad ideas. Find your local Gamblers, load up your whiskey, and tow straps and seek out trails and trash wherever they are to be found. Above all, stay rad and always be gambling.

Flenn Madarang poses on the hood of *The King* at OSO 2022, during a search for a hot spring marked out on our waypoint sheet. Those who know him are acutely aware that Flenn never misses an opportunity for a soak.

RECIPE FOR A GAMBLER

RESULTS MAY VARY

(NorCal Jess)

In a large bowl add:
2 cups kindness
1 cup send
3/4 cups good humor
1/2 cup hugs
1/4 cup zip ties and duct tape
3 tbsp love for shitboxes
1 tbsp love for nature
2 tsp hate for litterbugs
1 tsp navigational challenge
1/2 tsp Moondust
1 pinch lifted Miata
A sprinkle of vanholes

Mix with dirty hands until non-uniform consistency. Pour into an oil pan and bake at 350 for a weekend. Decorate with spray paint and stickers. Pairs best with campfires and Malört.

The Gambler 500 is known for many things. Culinary genius is not one of them. However, shovel tacos certainly do hit the spot after a long day on the trail.

GAMBLER GLOSSARY

A NOVICE'S GUIDE TO UNDERSTANDING WHAT THE HELL GAMBLERS ARE TALKING ABOUT

By Dustin DuBois

Rule Number 1	Don't be a dick.
ABG	Always be gambling, used the same way "aloha" is used in Hawaii.
Broken Garmin	The navigator is drunk.
Bronco	Any two-door SUV.
Cancelled	Doesn't mean anything.
Chancellor	Stephanie Nelson.
Cheater Class	Subarus, or non-Subarus, with working four-wheel drive and/or AC.
Christmas Lights	When every possible dash light is on and you aren't the least bit concerned.
Consult the Owner's Manual	Bang the rev limiter until the concerning noise either goes away or gets worse.
Coward Button	Brake pedal.
DBAD	A reminder to follow rule number one.
Doin' It for Dale	When you full, FULL send it. Extra double full sends.
Emotional Support Vehicle	Chase truck.
Fender Adjustment Tool	Rubber mallet (or a particularly girthy dildo).
Fiero	Any coupe or mid-engined car that is not a Pontiac Fiero.
Flying Cox/Dickbird	Offishul bird of the Gambler 500.
Full Send	Like regular send, but full. The kind of send that involves hopping in your shitbox with a leaking oil pan, rod knock and two functional gears and trying to jump a railroad track at full throttle.

Gambler Alarm Clock	Rev limiter of any variety, but almost always a Subaru.
GamFam	Your extended Gambler family.
Gambler Whiskey	The nectar of the Gods; smoother than Keith Stone himself.
Gibby	Any member of your team who generally makes the experience better but doesn't exactly contribute in a noticeable way. No one wants them to drive, they can't fix anything broken, probably won't cook a meal, but will always hand you a cocktail in a dire situation or get you a beer if you look thirsty or start swearing too much.
Glambling	Gambling with way-too-comfortable sleeping accommodations.
Godfather	Tate Morgan.
Hang Loose	To extend the arm out the window displaying a balled fist with thumb and pinky finger extended. Internationally recognized road greetings.
Horsepower	Stickers, or literal/fake horses on your vehicle.
Lava	Pavement.
Lejund	Someone everyone knows or should know; usually recognized by someone else that already has the status.
Life raft	Mini bike.
Love tap	Nerfing a fellow Gambler you don't yet know, as a way of saying hello.
Malört	Dreamsauce (Author's note: not recommended.)
Moondust	The gritty substance you will eat and find everywhere for years after leaving Chemult Gamblertown; makes an excellent dry-rub.
Mountain Money	Toilet paper.
OG	Oregon Gambler (also sometimes: Original Gambler).
OG88	Tribute to Jessi Combs.
OSO	Other Side of Oregon.
PUT IT IN THE KETCHUP!	The act of hitting the rev limiter.
Send	What you do to your shitbox, repeatedly.
Shitbox	Your car; no, don't be offended.
Sirch & Rascue	Not a typo.
Skinny Pedal	The one on the right, and the only one you should be using. Sometimes called the loud pedal.
Sunt	Past tense of send.
Supra	Honda Del Sol.
Team	Anyone driving in your group whether you know them or not, soon to be Gamfam.
Truck	Any pickup smaller than full size.
Ugga-dugga	Impact wrench.
Vanholes	Gamblers driving ballistic missile shitboxes.
Waypoints	Illegal substance.
Welder	Duct tape/zip ties.

This is what full send looks like.

3

STANLEY GAMBLERTON

TYLER HERDEN AND THE MONTERO OF DESTINY

OG Gambler

Our story begins before *Whiskey Business* was even a firing neuron in my brain. It started as a joke. A laugh. What if someone sends me some cash, and I build them a Gambler sight unseen, and they take it to the OG? Someone out of state flies in, and I hand them the keys. Whatever I conjure, they own. The first step was to see if there was interest. A Facebook post to the Gambler 500 Rally Group proved the idea had merit. The next was the budget. Being a car person and a Gambler, I know that you cannot purchase, title, and build a unique Gambler on an all-in $500 budget. It has been done, yes, but I couldn't bank on that. Just securing registration is half the budget. So we had interest and a rough idea of cost. I accepted that I would lose money. Keeping it Gambler means keeping it cheap, but despite budget constraints, I had to provide a reliable, unique vehicle.

Next, the victim. I knew from my pre-test that finding a participant wasn't going to be difficult. The issue would be finding the right person—someone easygoing, a little crazy, but also committed. This is still just an elaborate joke. The answer? A questionnaire! The questionnaire was provided to all those interested. I think within an hour I had ten responses. The questions were very deliberate. Nothing to do with cars, or even the Gambler. More like which Golden Girl is your favorite, and the specifics of peeing on a road trip. I filled out the questionnaire honestly, and then compared my answers with the others. The closest match would get first right of refusal.

Enter Tyler Herden. He wasn't the first, but he was closest to my answers. He also seemed most excited about the prospect. The offer was extended, and he accepted. We had our challenger. The established budget was $1,500. I also set aside $500 of my money, just in case. I asked Tyler a bunch of serious car questions, just to play into the joke. I had zero intention of actually using any of that info. I firmly believe that a car talks to you. When it's the right one, you know. However, messing with Tyler was half the adventure.

Tyler relaxes at his new bar. "There was so much for me to process, they had clearly put so much work into this for me. It was absolutely ridiculous, but amazing!" (*Stanley Gamblerton*)

Time to go shopping. I had half the money up front, which was good enough. Tyler said that he would fly into Oregon, drive the car, store it somewhere and fly home. The hope was that it would survive OG. So a mostly-reliable car was ok. I wanted to find him something fast-ish and loud. Maybe a beater Camaro, definitely V8. Eventually, I found the perfect car. Soon enough, parked in my shop was a beautiful Lincoln Mark VII. It was plush; a sea of leather and luxury. Smelled a little, but it's Oregon. Damp is a state of mind here. First thought: *Mad Max*. "The last of the V8 interceptors." I paid $800 for it, leaving plenty of the budget.

Plush also means saggy. This ol' girl was saggy. The pneumatic suspension stopped turning tricks when W. was still in office. It could probably do 500 fuel tank-dragging miles, but not much more. For the *Mad Max* theme, I bought armor from a retired prison transport. Whole truck load, cage included. We started putting the car together. Welding, trimming, it was all going swimmingly. Then the call came; Tyler had a change of plans. He now intended to fly in, Gamble all weekend, and then drive home—to Chicago. He wanted to make sure the car could survive the 2,000 miles.

By now he knew we had a car, but had no idea what. So like an idiot, I told him, "yeah, car can make it, no problem." Now this car was plush, it was cool, but it was not going to Gamble hard then drive all the way to Chicago. Back to square one, at this point I was

$900 in the hole. I had a car that I could run for the OG, but I didn't buy the Lincoln for me. I now had to buy a second car, with half the build time wasted. Cross-country-reliable cars don't typically cost $500. I had to get a $2,000 car for like $1,000, and fast.

After three weeks, I was about ready to say screw it, he's gonna Gamble a Lincoln that fills with smoke when you floor it. Plus he was like 5 feet 90 lb from Chicago. If he wanted to throw down, I'd take them odds. Enter the Montero of Destiny. I was browsing Craigslist and saw this vague advert for a totaled Mitsubishi Montero. It was shortened by about 23 inches in the rear after being hit. Front doors still opened, but everything else was bjorked. The seller bought it from the tow company for $700 and planned on parting it. The car was located 25 miles from the house, in the middle of literal nowhere, on back country roads. Don't get me wrong, this thing got hit hard in the butt. Yet when I put a battery in, it started right up. Not only that, it drove! Full tank of gas and all. Things were scraping and dragging, but it tracked straight and 4WD engaged.

Driving it home at night with one headlight was fun. No tail, brake or running lights either. It was, however, a low-mileage offroad machine. Everything cloth was spongy and moldy, but I managed to get it up to 80 mph on the way home. The Lincoln was rolled out, and the Montero was rolled in. First step: cut off the back. A little sawzall surgery, and we had our first look. One word: amazing. The wreck didn't even touch the frame! The Gambler gods gave us a high five that day. I was still a little miffed at now having two cars though. From that point on, I said to myself, "It will be reliable, it will be cool, but it won't be luxurious."

We removed everything that wasn't critical. Everything. I even took out the radio, just because. You don't need a radio to Gamble. Plus its only 2,000 miles to Chicago. You can hum. What we had was two doors and a steering wheel. It was back to square one for the theme; we now had about six feet of open frame to work with. So what does a twenty-something from Chicago need to meet new people at OG? A bar, of course!

Whiskey Business was born. An automotive mullet: business up front, party in the back. Not just any bar, it had to be classy. Our motivation came from Prohibition-era speakeasies. For the bar, I wanted something frame-mounted—heavy duty steel for the bar top and bench seat. I expected people to sit at the bar while he drove around. I also had an extra nice bench seat that fit well. We used pallets for the floor, and my old hand-made bar top became the bar. On it we put a sweet lamp for night drinking. The vehicle was called *Whiskey Business*, but the bar also needed a name. I happened to have two big metal roosters. Between those and the prohibition theme, we came up with the "Copper Cock." We painted the car in a metallic copper paint to look like an old moonshiner's still, then installed a cooler and used a washer fluid pump to make a liquor dispenser at the bar. A hidden switch, when pressed, would pump alcohol up through a lamp that I'd made from an old Austin valve cover. The lamp could spin, so you could angle it over the side of the car and pump libations straight into someone's mouth! My genius knows no limits.

This thing had dozens of little décor pieces to sell the theme. Since Tyler was going to drive this speakeasy across the U.S., I wanted to do something to guarantee he wouldn't get pulled over. Across the back I made a sign that said "Just Married." Nobody is gonna pull over someone on their honeymoon. The mud flaps did have male genitalia on them though. Now for seating: the stock seats weren't bad, but bitterness took over. Since this is an off-road machine, why not put some hard plastic seats in? May not be comfortable, but at least you won't slide around.

Tyler Herden says: "Stanley posted a video of him and his crew cutting everything off behind the SUV's B-pillar. The reason for this is because of a 'slight' ding, which looked to be the result of being rear-ended by a truck. So now I'm thinking 'I have a cut-up Mitsubishi on the other side of the country. This really is going to be an adventure.'" (*Tyler Herden*)

Tyler remembers: "Stanley told me to hold a shot glass under the lamp. I was confused, but went with it. All of a sudden he flips a switch under the bar, and out comes vodka. They literally built me a functional bar! I'm not normally one for shots, especially vodka, but I couldn't turn it down. I quickly realized that it wasn't vodka at all. It was gin. Now, taking a shot of gin is one thing, but taking a shot of gin *expecting vodka* will really catch you off guard." (*Stanley Gamblerton*)

How not to get pulled over in the American heartland, according to an Oregonian. (*Tyler Herden*)

Part of the agreement was we would provide basic camping gear. Since our budget was shot, we sent a guy out with $7. He found a kids pup tent and a super thin sleeping bag. The pup tent was maybe 4 feet wide. Perfect. I also felt obligated to at least stock the liquor dispenser with the first round. Quantity was key, so I went with something classy: a gallon of gin. Somewhere near the end of the build I traded the Lincoln for a 14-passenger van convertible—a vanvertible. That tale I'll save for another day. *Whiskey Business* was complete.

Enter Tyler Herden. Tyler was to fly in to Eugene the day before the OG. We would pick him up, and unveil his car. We met him at the airport with a sign that said something about getting my mother pregnant. I think. The unveiling was cool, and I feel he genuinely liked most of the vehicle.

Tyler's journey from that point on can only be told by him, or better yet, others, because he had drank a lot and had several blackout periods. I will share, though, a few highlights from our time together. First, the schwag. Imagine how cool it would be to get schwag for having a drink at the bar. Well, I hope your imagination is good, because that's all you get; Tyler left the bag of swag on the rear bench seat. Then he went for a drive, and lost it. He's been in Oregon thirty minutes and already littered. We called these things Tyler moments. There were plenty Tyler moments.

Next was liquor. He had gin, but if you have an open bar, you need to stock liquor. I took him to my local shop, where he bought one bottle of whiskey. Because Tyler

Tyler remembers: "Stanley had previously told me he had a treehouse I could sleep in. What I didn't know beforehand was that the bed in this treehouse was an actual toddler mattress. I made it work though, and it actually wasn't too uncomfortable." (*Tyler Herden*)

looks seventeen, the store owner made sure to card him. So I guess he's serving gin all weekend. That night we had planned to put him in my home bar. But my bar was already taken by my father-in-law. So instead of ruining the baby tent surprise early, we made him sleep in my kids' treehouse. As a joke, we put a toddler mattress up there. Jokes on us though, cause he fit fine.

I wish I could say that our journey to the OG went as smoothly as Tyler's. We wrecked into the side of a mountain once and broke down a lot. There was a moment when we broke down near LaPine and pushed our van-bus into a TacoBell parking lot. It had just started hailing, and we were getting tired of endless breakdowns. We were trying to get the van started; the battery was getting weak, so we swapped it between cars every so often to keep it charged. Once the van's engine turned over, you had to floor it to keep it running, then pound it into gear at full-rev or it would die. About ten minutes into our Taco Bell wrenching session, Tyler decided to go inside to drop a deuce. After he left, the van fired up. All cars ready, we need to roll now. Still no Tyler. It took him fifteen minutes to poop. He comes out looking all refreshed while we are all screaming. Tyler moments.

This was Tyler's first OG, but not ours, so we set up camp as far from the bullshit as possible. I'm too old for that. Tyler decided to abandon us and posted up at the entrance. From that point on, we only heard stories of Tyler. He faded off into Gambler legend.

Tyler says: "What Stanley had failed to mention to any of us was that the vanvertible's brakes were questionable at best. At one point, the van crashed into the side of a hill because the brakes stopped working, preventing him from slowing down enough to make a curve. Thankfully it happened when it did, because missing the next corner would have launched them down an embankment. We pulled over, bled the brakes and kept going." (*Tyler Herden*)

Tyler remembers: "While I can't promise you that letting strangers across the country build you a car is a good idea, for me, it was one of the best decisions I ever made." (*Tyler Herden*)

Tyler says: "It was bronze in color, had *Whiskey Business* written on both doors, and a sign on the back that read *Copper Cock Bar*. Why would a car have a sign saying that it's a bar?" (*Tyler Herden*)

The pallets are structural. (*Tyler Herden*)

Tyler remembers: "Both the van and the Saab had several breakdowns along the way, but they still made it to camp. Amazingly, the Mitsubishi didn't have a single issue. Little did I know just how reliable this wrecked, cut-in-half Montero really was." (*Tyler Herden*)

Tyler says: "Years later, I'm still blown away by just how much of an impact this car has had on my life. It has reliably carried me over 15,000 miles, through at least ten states. It has survived extreme heat, freezing cold, and triple-digit highway speeds without skipping a beat, and rescued more stuck vehicles than I can count. Somehow, it has never needed anything outside of the most basic maintenance. I would still trust it to take me cross-country with zero preparation." (*Tyler Herden*)

Above: Herden remembered: "I test drove it, and quickly realized that the bucket seats they'd installed were too low for me; I couldn't see over the dash. I ended up buying a pillow to sit on just to drive it." (*Tyler Herden*)

Right: Herden recalled: "To say that I felt anxious was an understatement; here I am, on the other side of the country with two strangers, going to see the car I'm going to have to drive back to Chicago." (*Tyler Herden*)

Above: Tyler has developed a well-earned reputation among his fellow Gamblers for his cheerful willingness to come to the aid of those in need. Fortunately for everyone else, Tyler's rugged Mitsubishi has yet to prevent him from rescuing those who don't have the good sense to fly across the country and sleep in a treehouse for half a car built by a guy with a flock of birds trained in the fine arts of torture. (*Tyler Herden*)

Left: In case you were wondering, Stanley Gamblerton looks exactly the way one would expect a guy called Stanley Gamblerton to look.

Above: The OG Gambler, being the original event, is where one can attain the greatest level of immersion into the chaotic, altruistic ridiculousness of the Gambler 500 community. From rare European sports cars to automotive Frankenstein creations straight out of Mad Max and everything in between, the OG Gambler is a sort of Burning Man for car enthusiasts.

Right: Michael Orr changes the decades-old oil in the Lancia Beta coupe that he and the author trailered to Central Oregon from southern California for OG 2022. This car had sat in a vineyard in wine country from 2001 to 2021. Coaxed back to life with a Chinese knockoff Weber carburetor and a new wiring harness, the bulk of the resurrection process was entirely cosmetic.

Jake McDonald and Casey Calia inspect Jake's Nissan Hardbody at OG 2019. The pair are dressed in appropriate attire for the location, the aptly named Camp Moondust. (*Nicole Poe*)

Although Tyler's rolling speakeasy is certainly innovative, it is far from the only rolling tavern one is likely to encounter at the OG Gambler, as this brewery-sponsored PT Cruiser readily demonstrates.

Clockwise from top left: Todd Clark, Tom Chemler, David Aparicio, and Doug Stairs decorate Doug's Nissan XTerra at OG 2022. Unlike a typical Gambler event, the bulk of the OG Gambler takes place in one sprawling camp, with waypoints for nearby garbage deposits in need of cleanup distributed to participants.

Each year's OG Gambler culminates in the passing of the OG Scepter from one champion to their hand-picked successor, generally someone who embodies the ideals of the Gambler and who has contributed to the community in a way that stands out. Pictured: 2022 winner Michael Shotwell.

Martini Racing livery spoofs are popular in the Gambler community.

One of the many wild creations one is likely to encounter at the OG Gambler.

It is not uncommon for people to trailer cars that are too impractical for a standard Gambler event to OG. However, this Reliant Robin has not only tackled several of Moab's sketchier 4×4 roads; it has been down a substantial portion of California's infamous Rubicon Trail as well.

4

NICOLE POE

ALWAYS FOLLOW STRANGERS WITH FREE CANDY INTO THE WOODS

Dirty Divas

Gambler never really "began" for me anywhere. I often felt like the odd one out in off-roading groups due to my budget building and just wanting to have fun. I didn't care about what parts you could afford, more where you could go and what you could do with your time in the woods.

I began an off-roading club in Oregon in 2017. Our focus was to teach people about trail fixes and good stewardship. Truthfully, I was just looking for somewhere I fit in. One winter day I was wandering along in the forest in Washington, scouting for an upcoming run. Suddenly, out of the woods came what looked to be a retired police car, siren wailing, with a large van chasing it. "Free candy" was scrawled along the side of the van. I was immediately intrigued. What kind of candy? Who was driving the van? And why were they chasing what looked like a disfigured version of my grandfather's old car? Where were they going? Could I go with them?

Later on, I pulled up to a ledge on the side of a mountain to get a better view down below. There, once again, were the speeding Ford and pursuit van. It seems they had found some friends, as they had been joined by a PT Cruiser with wheels that had no business being on a PT, a set of older Suburbans with color-coordinated paint jobs, and an onslaught of other wayward, hilarious vehicles. The Ford had stopped. It was stuck trying to pull itself up a slick hill of clay and mud. Free Candy, with no warning, decided to go ahead and give them a nudge, and proceeded to push the wailing Crown Victoria up the hill with no regard for either car.

I knew in that moment that I had to get in on this. It took me well over a year, but in 2019 I finally found these people. My people. The community that I had dreamed about finding was being built by dreamers, doers, make believers, artists, fabricators and stewards. That year I came across a page on Facebook, titled "Dirty Divas: Not Your Average Pillow Fight." Now, I had been to a few small events here and there, dipped my toes (and the muffler of my Jeep) in the water, so to speak. This run was an opportunity,

Nicole begins her personal journey toward becoming someone else's campfire legend. (*Nicole Poe*)

in my eyes, for my club to do some cool recovery and for us to meet and befriend rad women who wanted to be out in the woods like us.

I reached out, not expecting to get a response. I kept it simple, explained that I was offering recovery for the run, and only wanted to participate for the fun. Once in touch, I was given the address to a brewery not far from home and told what time to meet up to shake hands.

This is where my story takes an interesting turn. I arrived at the bar and, because I am terrified of new people, I stood there, having a chat and enjoying feeling like a total newcomer drooling over the ridiculous paint jobs. Suddenly, I heard my name from behind. I turned and found myself face to face with my best friend from high school, Willow, who I had not seen in well over a decade. Willow and I hugged for a solidly uncomfortable period of time before catching up. I found myself filled with joy just watching her face light up as she told me about all of the amazing people and things the Gambler had brought into her life. I was beyond excited at this point. I went home and proceeded to pack for three weeks.

Friday came sooner than I had expected. I awoke, double checked arrangements with my team, made sure I had enough food; coffee, a flat rack of eggs, camping gear, basic recovery equipment and all of my usual budget off-roading gear. We left with a single waypoint. We had no idea exactly how to find it, but Google Maps got us there after a few detours. It was dark at Friday camp; we would have missed it if not for the lightshow and random headlights buried in the woods off the gravel road. We posted up and I set about finishing a project I had brought with me: a stencil of the Divas logo.

Once that was done, I tucked it away and wandered about, too excited to sleep but too exhausted to do much of anything else. After a while, everyone bunked down. As the morning came, I found so many people, with so many stories I had already missed out

Driver's meetings at any given Gambler event are a spectacle all their own. Part carnival, part car show, part cautionary tale on the dangers of combining bourbon and a mig welder, any outside observer is bound to come away from the experience both curious and horrified. (*Nicole Poe*)

on being a part of. The fear of missing out was real. There were a few young ladies from southern California who had driven up in an all-red, mid-90s boat of a car. It wasn't starting, and a man I had never seen before, in a dress, was under the hood. This was Kevin Anderson, the legend himself.

I was in awe of the vehicles—spray-painted Broncos, a short bus, Jesse Jobe's PT Bruiser, a Mercedes with wings, a van with sponge-painted emblems … the cars alone made it somewhere I felt at home. People put their art out on their vehicles like I had never seen, and I was living for it.

As I was acquainting myself with a few folks, I was informed by B. J. Snyder that a celebrity who was super famous was in our midst. I tried to play it off, telling her he would get the same treatment from me as anyone else, but she made it very clear that this was simply not the case. He wanted the attention. He thrived on it. I had her point him out to me and give me his name, and from 50 feet off I screamed like I had just met Johnny Cash.

"OH MY GOD ITS GIBBY!" The sound of my fangirl screaming pierced the air. It set birds flying and caused everyone within earshot to stare at me like I had grown a third head. Thus began my perpetual torture of one of the sweetest men to have ever graced my presence. For years, every time I saw him, it was a fangirl scream, a hug, and asking him to autograph something ridiculous for me. In private, the conversations were always deeper, more about the projects we worked on together, the people we loved, and the people we didn't so much care for. But it always rang true between us that I was his number one fan from that day forward.

After a grueling Sunday of adventuring, I had to call it and missed the last few waypoints. I felt so guilty because I was always afraid someone was left behind, waiting

Kevin J. Anderson, SoCal's eponymous bowling ball magnet, shows off his little black dress while attempting to figure out what is wrong with a fellow Gambler's Cadillac. This being a car equipped with GM's unfortunate Northstar V8, the answer is, of course, everything. (*Nicole Poe*)

for us on the recovery team. We made it to camp and posted up. We had no idea that food was already handled; we had brought enough tacos to feed a small concert crowd. We made our food anyway, and offered it to everyone.

Some of us got drunk. Many of us had great conversations. I pulled a complete "mom" move and went to bed. After all, it was a rare moment that I was able to step away from my kids and just be free, and every mom dreams of that day, knowing her kids are safe, and what she would do with that free time. I found my answer: I slept like I hadn't in years.

Morning came and we gathered everyone together. We packed up camp and collected trash in the bed of a red truck. I spoke more with B. J. and Top Secret Stacy. I had found my people. They were in the woods, just like me. Doing rad stuff, just like me.

They gave me a trophy that weekend. I cherished it deeply and held onto it until I found someone I thought would love it as much as I did. It took a few years, but at Divas 3 it was passed on to M. B. for her epic skills at making everyone smile and being one of the most Gambler people ever.

I received the best gift in the world that weekend. I felt like I had finally found people I could proudly identify with, a tribe of my own. I belonged for the first time in my life. I was home.

Poe and several other Divas gather for a photograph in their natural habitat. Legend has it that Sasquatch himself took this photo in exchange for several cans of White Claw. (*Nicole Poe*)

Nicole poses with her trophy on the hood of her Jeep following her first gamble. She would go on to become a fixture at subsequent Dirty Divas runs, as well as a pillar of the larger Gambler community. (*Nicole Poe*)

If you're going to start a new life as a cryptid haunting the backwoods of the Pacific Northwest, it is important to look the part. (*Nicole Poe*)

Right: Every Gambler needs a slick paint job. Stencils and spray paint are a popular medium and are always readily available anywhere that Gamblers gather. (*Nicole Poe*)

Below: Sometimes two wheels are better than four, especially for those who enjoy feeling the wind blowing on their legs while their dress dangles perilously close to an exposed drive chain sprocket. Kevin, as always, is eager to discover a faster way to disrobe. (*Nicole Poe*)

Above: Nicole takes Gambling seriously. Rappelling down a steep cliff to pick up trash is not for the faint of heart.

Left: Nicole assists in diagnosing overheating issues with Harpoonigan, Speedfreak Speedshop's supercharged AMC Javelin.

Everyone at Gambler events is encouraged to pick up trash and help keep our public lands clean. Especially large pieces of trash are often documented proudly in the way that a fisherman might photograph his prized catch. Here Nicole poses with garbage that she reeled up from the depths of a steep ravine with the assistance of Doug Stairs.

Nicole Poe with Aja Rounds and two other Divas. In their element seated on dirt-spattered minibikes in the middle of nowhere, each of these women is a seasoned Gambler. (*Aja Rounds*)

Taking a break from slinging dirt for a glamor shot with an immaculately-decorated Crown Vic. The venerable Ford Panther platform is the workhorse of the Gambler 500. (*Nicole Poe*)

Proper Gambler driving attire includes a face covering and sunglasses or goggles. Both are invaluable when it comes to keeping out trail dust, a substance which will work its way through A/C vents, rust holes, and worn weather seals with the singular purpose of making breathing and seeing as difficult as possible. (*Nicole Poe*)

Diva and "Queen of Iceland" Xarene Eskander poses with her "Radillac," nicknamed *Dreki Blanco*. "The Dirty Divas run started as a nationwide conversation between like-minded women," says co-founder Stacy Dixon Kohon. In addition to their annual event held each May, a Dirty Divas flag flown over a cluster of cars or tents at any other event signifies a protected space in which any Gambler feeling threatened or vulnerable may seek refuge and aid. (*Nicole Poe*)

Men are typically allowed at Diva events on an invite-only basis, with the understanding that they should refrain from offering mechanical advice or assistance unless specifically called upon. This allows the women on whom the group is focused to gain valuable experience troubleshooting and fixing issues while building strong bonds with their fellow Gamblers. "We've tried to keep it around 51% female, if not more, which we accomplish by 'requiring' that all dudes come with at least one woman," says Divas co-founder B. J. Snyder. (*Nicole Poe*)

Right: Although most car problems a Gambler might encounter can be solved by simply turning up the radio, occasionally a more hands-on approach is required. (*Nicole Poe*)

Below: Diva icon and OG scepter winner Jessy Jobe pilots *PT Bruiser* down an old logging road. Incorporating a full-sized truck frame, supercharged small block V8 and most of a PT Cruiser, this unusual machine is as capable as any more conventional overland rig. (*Nicole Poe*)

Left: Several Gamblers at an Oregon Border Patrol event doing a "shotski." This involves a ski with ten shot glass-sized holes drilled in it, up to ten Gamblers, and a corresponding number of shots of the most vile liquor available. (*Nicole Poe*)

Below: Training the next generation of Gamblers in the art of stencil application. (*Nicole Poe*)

5

AJA ROUNDS

TERRIBLE HOOMANZ AT TEXAS CARNADO 2021

Texas Gambler 500

The story goes something like this: Mark Smith is an awesome person that I met through Gambler 500 who recently moved to Texas. Cody is a great friend of mine who also happens to live in northeast Texas. Mark decided to host an event, and I decided that this was an excellent excuse to visit Cody. Two of my teammates also have a great friend, Ismail, who lives in the Dallas-Fort Worth area. It was all pretty clear: we must go!

I found plane tickets for, like, $140; this is way cheaper than driving 2,300 miles cross country, and none of us can get that much time off work anyway. That meant we needed a car to gamble. I made a post on the Carnado event page and Kirk Popovici, whom we hadn't met yet, started helping us find a car. He made several calls and went to test drive things. I was very much in old man mode, so he found us *Marmalade*, a '91 Buick LeSabre with under 90,000 miles and a gamblin' attitude. It is amazing how a friend you haven't met yet can just appear in your life and go to great lengths to help you out! Kirk picked us up from the airport and brought us into his home. Once acquainted with our new car, we looked at all the issues and figured, "it's fine." We gave her an oil change, put some stickers on her, then took the day off to go do other fun Texas stuff.

Friday morning, we started rollin' and met up with our gamblin' caravan just over the border in Oklahoma to start heading to Gibby's biker camp. We set up camp and realized the UTV's fuse block was fried. We got to meet more of the Gamfam, stickered some cars, sang karaoke, and someone even snorted Malört! On Saturday morning, Gib and his cat delivered us burritos that Dall lovingly made. Then we readied ourselves to hit the trails. The UTV is still overheating at this point, even after J. B. (a new Gambler friend) saved us with wiring and connectors to reroute the melted fuses.

If you have ever rolled with us, you know we have a tendency to find "alternate routes." So we picked up trash and beat the shit out of our non-existent skid plates. I found out that boots are only waterproof if the water doesn't go over the top when we forded a river. We sent the troops over terrain so nasty it makes you happy to see lava

Marmalade, the '91 Buick. Standard features include top speed, upholstery, faux wire wheel covers, and an AARP membership. (*Aja Rounds*)

again and headed to camp for a beer afterwards. Back at camp, fed, and warming up in the RV, we heard a loud bang: it turned out the awning had collapsed for no reason. Then it started to snow. Marmalade was a beast offroad and it was my turn to drive, so we waited it out and removed the awning from the RV. By now it was 5 p.m. and people were returning to camp, so my shot at driving Marmalade on the trail was gone. Dall made us a nice stew for dinner and then the band started up, playing rockin' tunes for us all to enjoy by the bonfire with our new friends. On Sunday morning, Mark held a nice awards ceremony where we got to embarrass Kirk by publicly acknowledging his Gambliness. There's a lot more to the story, but dammit, I know y'all haven't even read all of this!

Suffice to say, Gamblers are awesome and I'll be back!

One of Aja's many talents is making friends. (*Aja Rounds*)

Aja and Flenn Madarang, dressed in their Sunday best, catch a ride up the hill at OSO 2022.

Aja and a cohort of Gamblers gathering trash at Beverly Dunes in Washington. Any Gambler will tell you that a minibike is the perfect vehicle for scouting out particularly remote dump sites. (*Aja Rounds*)

Breakdowns are relatively common at Gambler events, owing to the bulk of participants showing up in intentionally-bad cars. Fortunately, most Gamblers are capable field mechanics, in addition to being the types of people who will stop and help others when their own car is running semi-reliably. (*Aja Rounds*)

Aja exudes the cool, calm confidence of a woman who has been ignoring her flashing "check engine" light for months. (*Aja Rounds*)

Above: The Coleman Powersports minibike is a mainstay at Gambler events. Nimble, efficient, and loud enough to keep everyone in camp from sleeping, these rugged little workhorses are as at home roaming the open range as they are ferrying tired Gamblers to and from distant toilets at camp. (*Aja Rounds*)

Right: Speaking from firsthand experience, Aja is one of those people who tends to be the life of the party anywhere she goes. (*Aja Rounds*)

Above: What better way to explore the Washington backcountry than in a pair of boxy old Volkswagen Cabriolets? Sporty, stylish, and practical for a fraction of the price of a Jeep. (*Aja Rounds*)

Left: Is a VW Cabriolet of 1980s-vintage a good choice for a budget rally car? Aja seems to think so. (*Aja Rounds*)

Above: Being from the Pacific Northwest, Aja and the motley collection of Washington Gamblers pictured here are perfectly happy rambling around the woods knowing that the weather might turn on them at any moment. "Damp is a state of mind here," says Gambler and unfathomable entity Stanley Gamblerton. (*Aja Rounds*)

Right: To the extent that any Gambler event enforces a dress code, participants in the Lone Star State seemingly have even fewer requirements to adhere to. (*Poncho Cole*)

One of Aja's copilots, Elaine Louis, triumphantly shows off her hard-won garbage after retrieving it from a cactus patch in the Texas desert. (*Aja Rounds*)

Not content with simply yeeting around the wilderness picking up garbage, Aja can also be found at HooptieX races from time to time. (*Aja Rounds*)

Above: Anything can become a convertible with vision and a Sawzall, and Gamblers have a special gift for turning bad ideas into something more tangible. Fortunately, the first-generation Ford Explorer shown here is widely renowned as a stable platform not at all known for rolling over at the mere suggestion of a corner. (*Aja Rounds*)

Right: Even when she's completely by herself, Aja is the life of every party. (*Aja Rounds*)

Above: Texas' unique combination of vast tracts of uninhabited wilderness and highly-forgiving vehicle codes creates conditions for some incredible Gambler shenanigans. (*Poncho Cole*)

Left: Snow on the ground at Texas Gambler base camp. (*Poncho Cole*)

Right: A trophy for a Lone Star Gambler event. Due to its close proximity to Mexico, Texas Gambler routes sometimes include border crossings. Passports, though not required, are highly recommended. (*Poncho Cole*)

Below: A fourth-generation Camaro juxtaposed against the stunning backdrop of a Texas sunset. (*Poncho Cole*)

Two Gamblers taking a moment to admire the South Texas scenery. (*Poncho Cole*)

Above: West Texas is peppered with Border Patrol checkpoints. A Gambler convoy provides amusing relief from the tedium for officers at one such location. (*Poncho Cole*)

Right: Texas Gamblers clean up a scenic riverbank near Big Bend National Park. (*Poncho Cole*)

Left: A Gambler inspects his malaise-era Ford during a convoy stop. When traveling in packs, it is not unusual for a large number of Gambler cars to stop at once in the middle of the trail, generally to assist with repairs or clear out a large amount of garbage. (*Poncho Cole*)

Below: Gamblers are, by necessity, jacks of all trades. Any given Gambler participant will usually have at least a passable knowledge of basic automotive repair, metalworking, carpentry and creative use of J. B. Weld. Less common are esoteric skillsets such as rooftop martial arts, as demonstrated here. (*Poncho Cole*)

Above: An FJ80 series Land Cruiser and Mercedes ML take a breather in the hot Texas sun. (*Poncho Cole*)

Right: Out on the trail. Gamblers, especially those driving modified (or unmodified) passenger cars, often operate on the buddy system when far from civilization. This ensures that everyone has an extra set of hands, tools and, when all else fails, a viable escape option. It is also an excellent way to become acquainted with strangers. (*Poncho Cole*)

A convoy at rest, presumably to play with the chicken in the foreground. Gamblers are, by nature, both easily distracted and eager to make friends. (*Poncho Cole*)

Above: The Texas Gambler crew cool off in a cantina after a long day in the hot southwestern sun. (*Poncho Cole*)

Right: Mistakes were made, and presumably lessons learned. Rollovers at Gambler events are far from common, but they do happen. (*Poncho Cole*)

6

DILLAN LEU

WHAT'S A STATUTE OF LIMITATIONS?

Golden State Gambler

In 2017, I went pre-running and asked my cousin to join me for the day. I picked him up in the Subaru I'd bought earlier that year and we hit the dirt roads around the town of Arnold, CA. After chatting and driving for a few hours, we took a wrong turn. Looking at the map, I found that the road we were on wasn't marked, but I wanted to see where it went. Due to wildfires and the closure of the forest by Sierra Pacific Industries, after a few miles I decided to head back to the main road. I had planned on using that because as a major fire road it was definitely open.

On the way back to that main road, I took a smaller logging road covered in tall weeds. It didn't look like anybody had been there all year. I'm a bit of a slow driver, so puttering along I drove through a small wet area and the car started slowing down. I stopped and put it in reverse, almost backing out of it entirely. Then I put it in drive again and drove forward at the same slow speed, and that was it. I was stuck. It was about 4:30 p.m. Turns out I drove through a natural spring, so the ground was very wet around where the water ran. I had a come-along with me, but not enough tow strap to reach the nearest trees. We tried digging, but the car only sank more. We also tried finding pieces of wood and rocks to put under the tires, but after three hours, it started getting dark, the mosquitoes came out, and we gave up. We ended up sleeping in the car. We had very limited food and water.

The next morning, the car had sunk even more. We wrote a couple notes out of wood on either end of the trail and hiked towards a Cal Fire station that was a few miles away. Along the way, we spotted bear tracks. I happened to look up and watched a baby bear run across the road twenty yards ahead of us. Knowing that there's probably a mama bear around somewhere, we stopped and listened. We only had a dull hatchet and a stick for protection. Well, listening for Mama Bear to come kill us, I remembered a survival show about making noise to let animals know where you're at so you don't surprise them like we had with the baby bear. So we both grabbed sticks and started banging them together, continuing on our way.

Dillan's venerable green Forrester is, despite its relative lack of ornamentation by Gambler 500 standards, instantly recognizable to Gamblers across the western U.S. Generally, the last to roll into camp at the end of the day and the first to leave in search of lost or stricken friends, Dillan embodies the Gambler spirit like no other. (*Dillan Leu*)

The first-generation Subaru Forester is a much more capable car than appearances would have you believe. Unfortunately, even the indomitable Subaru symmetrical all-wheel drive has its limits. (*Dillan Leu*)

Have you ever seen a movie in which the hero, stranded on a desert island, signals passing aircraft for help by writing out a message using the surrounding environment? Yeah, that's actually a thing. (*Dillan Leu*)

The views are beautiful in the mountains of Northern California, but the woods are chock full of bears, mountain lions, Sasquatch, and a host of other predators that are best left to themselves. These mountains eat people. (*Dillan Leu*)

We arrived at the Cal Fire station about four hours after we left the Subaru, only to find nobody was home. I assumed they were out fighting fires, but thought maybe someone would come back. We explored the facility and played horseshoes for another couple of hours. That entire time, no vehicles drove by, marking a day and a half since we had seen another soul. The only vehicles there were the personal vehicles of the firefighters who were out fighting the wildfire. One of them, thank the Gambler gods, had left their keys in their truck. We had two options—either walk back to the main road where we might find civilization (probably be a 2–6-hour hike, plus the risk of bears and mountain lions) or we could borrow this guy's truck.

We proceeded to borrow his truck. It was one of the most stressful things I have ever done, so, being the nice guy that I am, I left a note made of rocks on one of the steps to the barracks: "Borrowed truck be back thx." A half hour of driving got us to my Subaru, where I accidentally roasted his clutch a little, but got us out. I drove the "borrowed" truck back to where we found it, my cousin following in the Subaru. It was a bit muddier than when we left. In it I left about $40 and a note thanking him and saying why I needed it.

From there, we headed out the way we came in, and now I always bring a buddy when pre-running. Most of the time.

Better to beg forgiveness than ask permission. In all likelihood, the keys to that truck were left in it for emergency purposes, such as allowing stranded civilians egress should the nearby wildfires spread this far. (*Dillan Leu*)

Sometimes you just need selectable four-wheel drive. Of course, opining as such borders on blasphemy in certain Gambler circles. (*Dillan Leu*)

Features such as ornate metal artwork and an outdoor barbecue area make life at this remote CalFire wilderness station seem almost idyllic. (*Dillan Leu*)

Despite being stuck up to its rocker panels in thick primordial sludge, Dillan's little Subaru survived the ordeal remarkably unscathed. (*Dillan Leu*)

Dillan, being one of the most polite human beings alive, was sure to leave a helpful note for anyone who might happen across his empty vehicle while he was away. (*Dillan Leu*)

Left: Dillan, affable as ever, posing at what has now become a crime scene. (*Dillan Leu*)

Below: Bear pawprints are nature's helpful reminder that humanity's position at the top of the food chain can be subject to change on a moment's notice. (*Dillan Leu*)

Dillan's idea of a road is somewhat more open-minded than most people's. (*Dillan Leu*)

With the durability to survive situations such as this, it is little wonder that Subaru is one of the most successful automakers in the United States. Among Gamblers, "Subaru" is almost always synonymous with "cheater." (*Dillan Leu*)

If you're going to bury your car up to the door sills in mud, at least do it somewhere pretty. (*Dillan Leu*)

There are fire roads, there are single-track roads, and then there's whatever this is. Anyone who has been on one of Dillan's routes can attest to the fact that he does not mess around when it comes to prerunning. The man has a penchant for challenging himself and his fellow Gamblers. (*Dillan Leu*)

Above: Dillan is one of two people at the helm of the Golden State Gambler 500. Encompassing all of Northern California, his events often include a staggering variety of attractions, such as ghost towns, hot springs, beaches, and several National Parks.

Right: Deep in the Sierra Nevada near the United States Marine Corps' Alpine Warfare Training Camp, Dillan, Chris Ruiz, and Poncho Backwoods compare navigational notes.

Pictured in Mendocino National Forest at Dillan's 2019 Coastal Carnage event is the author's own Mercedes 300D.

Halfway camp at GSG's 2019 Volcanic Venture Gambler, which crisscrossed across one of America's most underrated national parks.

Somewhere in the middle of nowhere, Calaveras County. Dillan has a singular talent for stringing together routes through the most spectacular scenery in Northern California.

Often overlooked yet invaluable to any Gambler event, Sirch & Rascue duty is generally voluntarily taken on by those possessing newer, more capable vehicles. Jeeps, full-sized pickups and truck-based SUVs are most common in this role. However, occasionally something more unorthodox, such as this four-wheel drive Porsche, can be found tugging someone out of a ravine.

Another rugged, capable European offroad machine, the W123 chassis Mercedes is a popular choice for Gamblers, especially those equipped with the venerable OM617 diesel. Although no longer as cheap as they once were, these Bavarian Brodozers still make an acceptable Pinzgauer alternative for those operating on a tight budget.

Drivers' meetings at Dillan's events are a fantastic opportunity for car spotting. This particular event saw representation for each of Germany's automakers. Chris Lee's black Audi Quattro, predictably, would end the event limping home from Mendocino to the Bay Area using a serpentine belt cobbled together from zip ties.

Occasionally, the cars themselves become the lejunds. Such is the case with Grant Innis' Mercedes 300TD saloon, nicknamed *Orca*, which has been gambling for almost five years as of this writing.

Another regular at Dillan's NorCal events is David Rudd, who can usually be found piloting *Ruddrunner*, his 4×4 chassis-swapped Plymouth Duster. On occasion though, it will turn up at the start line crammed into his dependable little Baja Bug.

Michael Orr stops to chat with the crew of the *Orca* during a navigational stop. The vast woodlands of Northern California are laughably easy to get lost in.

Though the W123 is an excellent choice for a Gambler build, finding one with the right powerplant can be tricky. This model, a 240D, is equipped with the least-ideal factory drivetrain—a naturally-aspirated four-cylinder diesel paired with an automatic transmission. Though fuel efficient, one could walk up a steep hill faster than this machine could carry them.

Occasionally, Dillan's faithful green Forester will be left at home in favor of his daily driver, the red Toyota Corolla at left. As one might expect, this does not diminish Dillan's ability to have fun on the trail at all.

Alex Janik, Matt Parrot, and Flenn Madarang attempt to figure out why Alex's Blazer will not retain coolant. Eventually, Alex and his codriver Ian determined that there was a break in one of the cooling hoses. The pair proceeded to drive the truck over one of the highest mountain passes in the Sierra Nevada and back again a day later, stopping every fifteen minutes to refill the cooling system from the many alpine streams along the side of the road.

Air-cooled Volkswagens are popular with those Gamblers who enjoy life at a slower pace. Though Microbus prices have risen astronomically over the last twenty years, several can still be found rambling down old logging trails at the back of a Gambler convoy.

7

FLENN MADARANG

A PERFECTLY ORDINARY ROAD TRIP THROUGH THE DESERT

Everywhere

It all started when I went to meet up with Felixx for Hot August Nights in Reno. He was going to be late, and I'm just dragging ass. It is fine. When we get there its Saturday, and we realize that Hot August Nights isn't in Reno that weekend; it is in Virginia City. That's an hour out of our way, so I said to Felixx, "Hey man, why don't we just enjoy what we've got? We've already got a hotel here."

There was a hot wing festival. Reno was having its annual hot wing festival. Meanwhile, I had booked us into the sketchiest hotel on the Reno strip. When we got there, there was an ambulance call, police streaming in. I watched some guy get resuscitated after overdosing on something in his hotel room. We were just sitting in the Escalade like, "We're just gonna soak in this atmosphere," cracking open White Claws and having a great time waiting to check in. We did the hot wing festival; it was whatever. The next day, I opened up the schedule for Hot August Nights and it showed Friday, Saturday—today was Sunday—Monday, Tuesday, Wednesday. There's nothing in line for the first Sunday of this two-week festival.

Still, we made our way to Virginia City, cause why not? We spent the day in the nice little ghost town. Although we saw a few classic cars, it wasn't packed. So we left Virginia City and started heading south, towards Area 51, and that's where shit hit the fan.

We passed the largest army base and ammo depot in Nevada, and as we headed through Tonopah, we started getting torrential rains. It was so bad that I could not see the car in front of me. We managed to get ahead of the storm by about fifteen minutes by the time we stopped in Tonopah for gas and food. I knew of a hot spring nearby, so we got back on the road and tried to stay ahead of the storm. It sprinkled on us a bit, and if anything was foreshadowing what would happen next, it was that. We got to the hot spring, we beat the storm, but it was still coming for us. We didn't know it at the time, though, so for now we got to enjoy this whole abandoned restaurant, bar, and hot spring complex with only wild cows for company. It was a good time.

Flenn has developed a reputation in the Gambler community as a fashion innovator. It is exceptionally rare to see him in the same outfit twice.

I started getting out as it started sprinkling, and I suggested to Felixx that we make for Area 51 before things got worse. He proposed instead that we should stay and enjoy the experience of torrential rain and the hot spring at the same time. I decided he was right. Soon it started coming down, then it started really coming down. I noticed the hot spring source water coming into the pool was going from clear to muddy to a silty flash flood. It wasn't even hot water anymore.

We were parked across the street, diagonally from the hot spring. We had to cross through a flooded, slippery drainage ditch to get back to the car. We started heading down Highway 375, the Extraterrestrial Highway, towards Area 51. The water was starting to drown parts of the road; it was a few feet deep in places. Eventually, it got to where the road alternated between sections of built-up silt and deep water. After a while, we had to stop for a Prius that had gotten stuck in front of us and a truck pulling him out. While we waited, we chatted with some locals, who informed us that snowplows would make their way through "eventually." Two Nevada State Troopers just laughed and told us, "good luck" when I asked them about road clearing.

As we headed back down the road, I noticed that something in the drivetrain was making a funny sound. We kept going, through water crossings that had mostly drained by this point. About 10 miles from Rachel, Nevada, we decided to stop between two mountains to take in a gorgeous view of the night sky, and also to take a bathroom break. We never made it to town. When I started the car and shifted from park to drive, it was just grinding. I shifted to neutral, then to reverse. More grinding.

"Hey Felixx, I think we have six neutrals."

Above left: Flenn enjoying a soak in the suspiciously-developed hot spring that he and Felix discovered deep in the Nevada desert. (*Flenn Madarang*)

Above right: One of several abandoned buildings near the hot spring. This humble shack has likely stood for at least a century, judging by its stacked stone walls and rough-hewn timbers. (*Flenn Madarang*)

In the end, we decided to camp there. That night got really weird and creepy. You know how crickets sound, right? I've never heard a fake cricket in my life 'til now. These only made half the sound that a normal cricket does, and then just held that note. Government insect drones from Area 51. You heard it here first! I finally got some sleep, which was a problem for Felixx because apparently I snore. Of course, I don't notice; I'm asleep.

The next morning, we consulted the owner's manual, which doesn't cover what to do when you have six neutrals. We were drawing straws to figure out who was going to hitchhike into town when a passerby stopped for us. He wore driving gloves, had a black trash bag over the driver's seat, and carried an empty cooler in the back. He was super kind and took us 200 miles. He was an old-school Mormon who spent the whole ride telling us about his life—a great guy, although I got the feeling that if only one of us had gotten in his car, we wouldn't have made it back alive.

In Saint George, Utah, we got a rental truck and headed back into Nevada to get our car. In Rachel, we asked around the town of forty-six residents trying to find a tow

Although reflective jackets and helmets are certainly a wise choice as far as minibike riding gear is concerned, Flenn never misses an opportunity to go above and beyond.

strap. In the end, we were able to find a section of chain, and flat-towed the Cadillac 10 miles into town. The chain broke once, so we tied it in a knot. We left the Caddy in front of the iconic Little A-Lee-Inn motel for the next four days. AAA was unhelpful as always, so the locals banded together and helped us get a tow back to Saint George. We dropped the car off at a garage on a Friday night and got dinner before getting back on the road. Now we were headed for Sturgis, South Dakota, sixteen hours away.

Since Felixx was too tired to drive, I decided to one-shot that last stretch. About the twelve-hour mark, I felt like I didn't have arms. I kept driving. We stopped by Devil's Tower in Wyoming, where I got my second wind. We hit Sturgis at about 10 a.m., just as everyone is waking up. We were there for less than 24 hours, and a lot of it is a blur. I took nine days off to get to Sturgis to spend less than a day there. It was a great time though; I'd definitely do it again.

Flenn Madarang and Felixx Johnson are often travel buddies to and from Gambler events. The pair are about as tight-knit as Gambler gets. (*Flenn Madarang*)

Felixx Johnson attempting to stay warm at OSO 2022.

Felixx with Gambler Lejund C. J. Cromwell, his jetski-bodied motorcycle, and two unknown acquaintances at Sturgis Motorcycle Rally 2022. The world-famous event draws thousands of bikers to the small South Dakota town every summer. In recent years, a sizable number of Gamblers have begun to appear alongside them. (*Flenn Madarang*)

Opposite page: More Sturgis shenanigans. The annual festival has an energy to it which many Gamblers find particularly inviting. (*Flenn Madarang*)

Left: One of Flenn's most valuable skills is his ability to feed himself using only what the environment provides. In addition to being an expert mushroom forager, he is also a capable fisherman. Of course, it helps when the fish are just lying on a riverbank.

Below: Another view of the terrain surrounding Flenn and Felixx's hot spring. The low, moist soil and toppled trees make it very clear that this area is within the path of floodwaters during heavy downpours. (*Flenn Madarang*)

Flenn poses with Matt Biles on the 2021 Central Coast Gambler. Their car would lose a bumper and wrap up its engine wiring harness in one of the front wheels before the weekend was over.

After getting his MX5 roadster stuck in deep sand just feet from the rapidly rising tide, Flenn airs down his tires while Matt Alber takes advantage of the photo opportunity. This trip would eventually wind up as the subject of a sensationalized news editorial regarding the growing popularity of this particular beach.

Left: Bare legs in booty shorts poking out from underneath a broken Miata is a common sight at any Gambler halfway camp in the western U.S.

Below: Wherever Flenn goes, his faithful pup, Pia, is never far behind.

Right: Flenn's infamous Miata parked at the Trona Pinnacles, April 2021. Earlier in the day, the rugged little sports car came in third in a dry lakebed drag race between it and the two ponderous luxury sedans parked alongside.

Below: Despite being possibly the only human in history to make a habit of sleeping on the roof of a Miata, Flenn is not immune to the types of rude awakening common wherever Gamblers congregate.

Flenn is almost singlehandedly responsible for starting the all-weather hot pants trend which has taken the Gambler by storm.

Flenn cools off in a portable pool near Trona, California during the awards ceremony for the 2021 Fool's Gold SoCal Gambler. (*Doug Stairs*)

Flenn and Pia relax in the backseat of Doug Stairs' (*right*) Nissan XTerra on a sojourn across a dry lakebed in California's Johnson Valley. Meanwhile, Matt Biles (*left*) attempts to decipher their waypoints sheet. (*Doug Stairs*)

A large gathering of NorCal Gamblers at the final waypoint of the 2021 Golden State Gambler Spring event. Flenn and his battered Miata are joined by "NorCal" Jess Wagoner in her Mitsubishi Raider, Michael Orr in his E Class Mercedes diesel, Brian Orr's rally-prepped Volvo, Doug Stairs' XTerra, David Rudd's *Ruddrunner* and a cohort of other jalopies.

Above: Attempting repairs to the steering mechanism of his Miata after sinking it on a remote beach along California's Lost Coast. The bent bracket holding the steering rack in place was eventually corrected using a large rock and a crescent wrench.

Right: Almost finished fixing the steering. This particular event wasn't even a Gambler; a bunch of people who happened to be Gamblers just decided to go camping one weekend.

Left: Waste not, want not! Flenn's foraging skills on the way home from OSO 2021 returned a set of lightly-used hooves, which he then ziptied to the author's truck while he wasn't looking.

Below: Gamblers at Sturgis. C. J. Cromwell, seated on his "Jetskicycle," appears unimpressed by the motorized sofa overtaking him. (*C. J. Cromwell*)

Right: Flenn has spent a decent amount of his gambling career hitching rides to and from events. Such was the case at the end of OSO 2022, when he rode home from Ukiah, Oregon with the author. After popping a thrift store Journey cassette into the tape deck, he immediately fell asleep for three hours.

Below: James Bates tows Flenn across a deep river crossing at the 2021 BFD Father's Day Gamble. Incredibly, the intrepid little roadster survived the ordeal without hydrolocking its miniscule 1.6-liter engine.

Freshly-coated in central Oregon mud following some hot laps in his go-kart, Flenn has a chat with Indiana Allison.

Above: It is a rare thing to see Flenn sleeping somewhere comfortable.

Right: Modeling his bold fashion choices in the woods of Northern California. Aprons of all varieties are a particular favorite of Flenn's.

Flenn and several fellow Gamblers take a break to cool off in a stream on a hot summer morning somewhere in Tahoe National Forest. At this particular event, Flenn stopped to bathe in nearly every body of water along the planned route.

Elements of the Bates family take a moment to instruct Flenn in the proper use of a personal floatation device.

8

NOAH ECKHOUS

HOW NOT TO USE SELF-TAPPING SCREWS

Gambler 500 SoCal

SoCal Gambler, The Gibson 500. Lucerne Valley, California. Fall 2021. It was two weeks before what would be my first Gambler. After years of close calls, I decided I was going to make this one happen. I'm always looking at shitboxes online, so when my friend posted his car for sale on social media, I hit him up. Later that day, I was the proud new owner of a 2001 Honda Accord. This thing needed help if it was going to survive. I really felt the Gambler spirit. I'm fortunate to have a willing friend with a welder and a scrap pile; I drove the car up the next weekend and we spent two days armoring the front end. We built a bumper from square tube and ¼-inch plate to protect the radiator and then two more ¼-inch plates welded to the front subframe to protect everything else important. We were ready to skid to the finish line if we had to.

I turned around and drove it back to Long Beach to prepare for the next weekend. With tools, fluids, and four bodies on board, the sag was godawful, but it rode great on the freeway. Offroad, it was smooth, but bottomed out frequently. The first half of the first day went off without a hitch. We found a group to travel with and were bringing up the rear, scraping most of the way to the first few checkpoints. We made it to the shooting gallery checkpoint and there was more trash than we could've hoped to pull out. After filling several contractor bags and hardly making a dent, we were feeling pitiful. We picked up an old F-100 fender and looked at our car, trying to figure out where we could mount it, eventually settling on the hood. We would just load it up with self-tapping sheet metal screws. Once we decided to go for it, we were feeling ourselves and added two more discarded hoods and a 2.5-gal refrigerant cylinder.

After a trail fix—Keith Shaffner's Crown Vic needed a new upper control arm—we got back on the trail with our trophies. We didn't account for the added height of the steel and found ourselves driving with our heads out the window in order to spot and avoid obstacles. Fortunately, my friend that was driving was tall enough to make do. We ended up on the highway for a bit, thankfully failing to attract any attention. Several hours later, we rolled into camp after being jostled thoroughly for most of that time.

Right: Noah and his long-suffering Honda Accord. Note the large amount of garbage he and his teammates have attached to the hood using sheet metal screws.

Below: When operating an overloaded sedan at stock ride height on rocky terrain, it pays to invest in some beefy armor for the car's tender bits.

The next morning, we reconfigured, moving the cylinder to the roof and stomping the sheet metal into compliance. After getting it all fairly flat, we attached it with a few self-tappers and we were off for another day of abusing our small sedan. This day we wanted to push the limits, having had no issues on day one. We eventually found our match in some deep sand and were quickly buried up to the expansive skid plate. Some lovely strangers gave us a tug, but to no avail. Sirch & Rascue folks showed up shortly thereafter and had more success. We made it out of the dunes and proceeded to Goliath's "Finger" after a stop at Cougar Butte's. Our approach to the Finger was unorthodox; we dropped down a long, loose slope and crossed a series of steep embankments on our approach until it became untenable. We turned around and did some joyriding in this area until a friend high-centered us on a mostly buried boulder. We all gathered around and rocked the car back and forth until it could drag itself off. I was in front for the final push, weighing down and trying to balance on the bumper. As soon as he got traction, I fell right onto the bullet-perforated sheet metal screwed to the hood. I peeled myself off with only a few puncture wounds, glad that I was up to date on my tetanus vaccine.

Noah and crew attempt to free their stricken sedan from soft sand. Despite operating in a primarily desert environment, such rescue efforts are a common sight at SoCal Gambler events.

After four attempts smashing into the slope, we descended to get to this point; we were then able to crawl up and back to the highway. The adrenaline wearing off after unifying with the rusty hood briefly, I was enjoying the freshly paved road and not being thrown around for the first time in hours. Approaching 70 mph, we were cruising and recovering from the weekend's activities. Suddenly there was a huge whoomp and my vision went black briefly. While I was trying to figure out what the fuck happened, I noticed my visibility had improved drastically. That's when it clicked—all of our hood ornaments had ripped free in unison and flew nearly 40 feet in the air before smashing into the tarmac. Our radio chirped confirmation from the cars following us and the caravan pulled over. We circled back and recovered the projectiles. Somehow, they had missed everything attached to the roof, as well as our fellows who happened to be trailing at a sufficiently healthy distance.

One last time, with more screws, we reattached the trash and returned it to civilization where we could dispose of it properly.

Having further encumbered their Honda with several large pieces of scrap metal, the Accord crew and other Gamblers in their caravan assist Keith Shaffner in repairing his Crown Victoria's broken front suspension.

Left: A snapped upper control arm on Keith Shaffner's Ford forced the convoy to stop and undertake repairs. Keith, who breaks something nearly every time he starts his car, carries spare control arms for exactly this reason. This would be the second one to snap in 2021.

Below: Trail repairs are underway. Noah assisted repair crews by presenting a curated playlist consisting almost entirely of songs by the Toilet Bowl Cleaners.

The Honda's crew poses for a photograph with their plucky steed.

Above: Though the Accord was far from the only Honda at that event, Noah's crew had modified their car considerably less than some.

Left: Pausing to help others in the caravan cut more metal out of their fenders is widely considered the polite thing to do.

Noah and company doing some last-minute prep at Café 247 before heading off into the desert. Located in the middle of nowhere, the remote eatery is the starting point for the majority of SoCal Gambler events.

Another member of Noah's ad-hoc convoy was Joe Komenda in his Subaru wagon, nicknamed *Cecil the Racecar*.

Iowan Adam Witthauer and his copilot cannonballed halfway across the U.S. in a truly mangled S10 Blazer for the 2022 Spring SoCal Gambler. Following the event's conclusion on a Sunday afternoon, they drove nonstop to reach home before Adam had to be at work the following Tuesday. The duo earned the event's scepter for their trouble.

Ian Malone and Alex Janik's troublesome S10 Blazer became stuck in deep primordial mud in the Anzo Borrego Desert. Fortunately for them, Keith Shaffner had brought 40 feet worth of tow straps. The two were eventually yanked free.

Keith Shaffner, Adam Witthauer, and the author stop to determine whether or not to proceed past an unexploded ordnance warning sign after cresting a difficult set of dunes.

Sunsets in the California desert are a spectacular sight. The unimaginably vast emptiness makes for ideal camping conditions, especially during the cooler months.

The King, *Jaggernaut*, and *Mercules Mk III* gather on the shores of the Salton Sea before heading into the desert. Each car is a Gambler lejund in its own right, veterans of years' worth of events. Over the years, all have been passed down from their original builders to eager new owners at least once.

Above: Though not as ubiquitous as it's W123 stablemate, the W126 S Class is quickly gaining popularity among Gamblers for its durability, comfort and ease of maintenance. Pictured is *Mercules Mk III*, the third car to carry the *Mercules* name. Like its predecessors, it is powered by Mercedes' venerable OM617 turbodiesel and has been outfitted with oversized all-terrain tires.

Right: Gary Requa assists in the removal of damaged parts from the Gibson family's BMW. Once the personal conveyance of Gibby himself, the rugged 5 Series was handed down to his niece and nephew after his tragic passing.

Alex Janik and Adam Witthauer assist two fellow Gamblers with jury-rigging a solution to their broken alternator mount. Like several others in their convoy, this Geo became stuck in deep mud. Unlike every other car present, however, the diminutive hatchback was able to be pulled free by the combined efforts of several large men.

Kostya Marowitz, known by his fellow Gamblers as the "Mad Russian," shows off the impressive front suspension travel of his Lexus LS400.

C. J. Cromwell inspects *Trophy Mutt* during a stop in the abandoned tungsten mining town of Atolia in 2019. The heavily-customized Chevy Tracker is one of the Gambler's most recognizable rigs; it has featured in off road expositions, tough truck challenges and various other non-Gambler events across the U.S.

Halfway camp at SoCal's High Desert Hangover event in 2019. Gambler veterans with a keen eye will spot several well-traveled rigs scattered about camp.

The early morning sun rises on a menagerie of hoopties near Randsburg, California.

Right: Enjoying the views in the desert near Trona, California, with the *Stinkin' Lincoln* in the foreground. The 1987 Continental came to reside in California at the end of the 2018 *Route Sucky-Suck* Lemons Rally, and was the author's Gambler conveyance for the 2021 season.

Below: Melody Liu and Maximilian Putintsev's W123 Mercedes basks in the early morning sun near the Salton Sea. Like almost all Gamblers who choose an older Mercedes diesel, they have sacrificed outright speed for nigh-indestructible build quality. Their humble E Class has entirely shrugged off damage which would cripple most ordinary cars.

Michael Orr patches *Jaggernaut*'s damaged oil pan with quick-setting epoxy at the SoCal Out of Bounds event in the fall of 2022. Though now powered by a GM small block V8, the sleek British touring car has managed to retain Jaguar's famed reliability despite the loss of its former V12 mill.

Right: Michael Shotwell's Mercedes ML, *Elk Punter*, pulled up alongside *Jaggernaut* under the abandoned Eagle Mountain Railroad trestle near Desert Center, California. Shotwell, the 2022 OG scepter holder, has piloted the tenacious little SUV through forty-nine out of fifty states. Wearing stickers and dents from countless Gambler events, *Elk Punter* has racked up nearly half a million miles.

Below: A Gambler negotiates a steep descent at the 2019 High Desert Hangover event.

Left: Michael Orr consults the map in the passenger seat of the first *Mercules* in the ruins of Atolia. The former tungsten mine is a frequent stop on SoCal Gambler routes, as it is the nexus point for several branching trails leading away into the desert.

Below: Noah Eckhous's teammates look on as he makes adjustments to their front skid plate.

Right: Late arrival at halfway camp, viewed from the cabin of the author's Dodge Dakota. Auxiliary driving lights are one of the most common modifications one is likely to spot on a Gambler car, and for good reason.

Below: Casey Albrite and his copilot relax in a remote hot spring in the shadow of the Providence Mountains. Though it is still an arduous journey to reach them, the undeveloped hot springs at the bottom of this valley have exploded in popularity in recent years due to social media and the booming popularity of outdoor recreation in the U.S.

ADDITIONAL READING

More information about the Gambler 500, its history, and the people who make it such a dynamic and thriving automotive subculture can be found here:

Bowman, Z. and Linquist, J., "Go Down Gambling," *Iron and Air Magazine* Issue 31, ironandair.com/winter-gambler-500/

Burns, G., *Detroit Gambler 500, A Rustbucket Rally for Weirdos, to Sputter across Michigan* (mlive.com, 2017), mlive.com/news/detroit/2017/04/the_detroit_gambler_500_a_rall.html

Elkin, J., *2022 Gambler 500 Shatters Trash Collection Record* (OffRoadXTreme.com, 2022), offroadxtreme.com/event-coverage/2022-gambler-500-shatters-trash-collection-record/

Gambler 500, gambler500.com/

Streeter, M., "How Offroading a Smart for Two Completely Changed My Life," *The Autopian* (2022), theautopian.com/how-off-roading-a-smart-fortwo-completely-changed-my-life/